CAREER AS AN

I0488283

ACCOUNTANT

ACCOUNTING IS ONE OF THE MOST in-demand careers today, with more new jobs opening up every day. The opportunities available to accountants, auditors and similar professionals in the field are expected to continue expanding as international business increases and more government regulations take effect. Accounting is rated among the top five careers by such publications as Forbes and CNN/Money, with new graduates earning an average of $55,000 in their first year on the job.

Accountants work with businesses, governments and other organizations to analyze and manage their finances. Accountants use spreadsheets and other computer applications to record, communicate and interpret financial results. They track transactions, recommend cost-cutting measures, and ensure that taxes are paid promptly and correctly. Accountants also help individuals and families file their taxes and manage their personal finances.

Opportunities for accountants can be found in cities of all sizes across the country. Some accountants are employed directly by businesses, government agencies, not-for-profits, colleges and similar organizations. Others work for public accounting firms that are retained by organizations to provide financial services. Accountants may also be self-employed, such as those who specialize in providing tax services for families.

A four-year degree from an accredited college or university is typically the minimum requirement to land your first job as an accountant. A graduate degree can be helpful, particularly for management positions or highly technical financial analysis work.

Many accountants obtain professional licenses, most notable the Certified Public Accountant (CPA). State licensing requirements vary, but CPAs generally must obtain additional college credit hours, have experience working in the field, and pass a rigorous examination.

Employment experts predict that the number of accounting and auditing jobs will grow by over 15 percent within the coming decade, as economic expansion drives the need for financial expertise.

Accountants and auditors are paid on average $65,000 a year, a significant increase from just $60,000 only a few years ago, and earnings are expected to continue to track upward.

Accountancy calls for sound skills in mathematics, analytical thinking and problem-solving. Accountants spend much of their time at computer screens, reviewing spreadsheets and analyzing financial data. Good written and spoken communications skills are important, because accountants prepare reports and present their findings to clients and upper management. They also need strong observation skills that help them pay close attention to details.

If you have good analytical, interpersonal, and mathematical skills, you can build a rewarding career as an accountant. The hours can be long and the work is sometimes tedious. However, through proper training and hard work, you can achieve the personal and professional satisfaction that many accountants enjoy.

WHAT YOU CAN DO NOW

IF ACCOUNTING SOUNDS LIKE AN INTERESTING career, start taking those first steps now to prepare for the profession. High school classes in mathematics, statistics, general business and accounting itself will give you a good start. Sound computer skills are highly useful, as accountants use spreadsheets, financial databases and word processing software. Take a keyboarding class and learn how to use tools such as the Microsoft Office Suite (particularly Excel, the spreadsheet application). Look for courses at your school, online, and at local colleges.

Learn more about the profession by reading industry publications in your library or online, such as *New Accountant*, which targets newcomers to the profession. Visit the websites of professional associations such as the American Accounting Association or the National Society of Accountants. Some organizations have local chapters and regular meetings, so you may be able to visit a session or obtain a student membership. Networking with working accountants helps you learn about local scholarships, internships, and entry-level jobs.

Set aside a couple of hours to talk directly with a working accountant. Interviewing someone who does the job on a day-to-day basis provides a real-world view of the rewards and challenges of accounting. You can find these professionals through family contacts, professional organizations, civic clubs, your high school guidance counselor, or by searching online.

HISTORY OF THE PROFESSION

WHILE THE FORMALLY RECOGNIZED profession of accountancy is less than 200 years old, accounting practices and principles date back thousands of years. The earliest civilizations developed systems and tools for keeping financial records, exchanging goods for currency, conducting international trade, and collecting taxes from their citizens. Accountants are credited with developing the written word, plus creating the financial platforms that allowed international commerce and business to flourish.

As early as 7500 BC, people kept track of agricultural and livestock trade by using tokens (an early type of currency which was replaced by coins around 700 BC). Early accountants developed writing systems around 3200 BC, using clay tablets, papyrus scrolls and other methods to keep track of inventory and taxes. The Code of Hammurabi (about 2200 BC) included laws covering commercial transactions and contracts. The Phoenicians created an alphabet to document their trade with Egypt. The Egyptians invented the abacus for complex calculations. Auditors were introduced in 423 BC to verify the contents of warehouses. The first banking system arose in Greece around 575 BC, with bankers taking metal coins as deposits and making loans. The Roman Empire built on those earlier innovations, as well as introducing legal corporations, land and sales taxes, and more complex financial systems.

The modern system of accounting arose in Italy, which emerged as the center of European banking during the Dark Ages. Italy was strategically located to facilitate trade between England, continental Europe and the Far East. The country's bankers also helped the leaders of the Crusades raise money to finance their armies. This high level of financial activity demanded more sophisticated bookkeeping procedures. Luca Pacioli, "the father of accounting," wrote a treatise in 1494 that detailed double-entry accounting. Double entry allowed merchants to more efficiently maintain financial records and gain a clearer picture of their businesses. Double-entry accounting was actually devised around 1300, but Pacioli's book – one of the first printed on Johannes Gutenberg's moveable type printing press – popularized the practice globally and set accounting standards that remained largely unchanged for the next 500 years.

Radical changes took place in accounting systems beginning with the Industrial Revolution. Railroads, iron and steel manufacturers, international trading companies, and other large-scale industries drove the development of capital investments, dividends, stock exchanges, public companies, and other modern structures. These new business models required sophisticated accounting systems to audit the enterprises and track their financial activities. In 1845, William Deloitte opened an accounting firm which grew into

Deloitte & Touche, one of the original "Big Eight" accounting firms that dominated the global accounting industry through the end of the 20th century.

In 1854, accounting became a formally recognized profession in Scotland when two organizations received royal charters: the Edinburgh Society of Accountants and the Glasgow Institute of Accountants and Actuaries. Both groups decided to call their members "chartered accountants," sparking dozens of similar organizations around the world. In 1887, 31 accountants created the American Association of Public Accountants (AAPA). The AAPA devised the first standardized tests for accountants and issued the first CPA licenses in 1896.

During the 20th century, political events were the main drivers in changes in the accounting profession. The Great Depression that began in late 1929 spurred legislation that reformed the banking and investment systems, including creating the Securities and Exchange Commission in 1933. The regulation of financial markets aimed to eliminate fraud from the marketplace, and led to corporate standards that became known as Generally Accepted Accounting Principles (GAAP). Several boards oversaw the accounting standards over the decades, with the Financial Accounting Standards Board (FASB) taking over in 1973.

World War II saw the US government expand the role of income taxes as its main source of revenue, spurring the need for accountants who could help families and corporations file their tax returns and find legitimate ways to reduce their tax bills.

In the early 21st Century, a series of accounting scandals at major US corporations brought more changes to the accounting world. The collapse of Enron (along with similar collapses of such companies as Worldcom, Tyco and Adelphia) led Congress to pass the Sarbanes-Oxley Act of 2002. The SOX act introduced new regulations and set new standards for accounting firms, corporate boards of directors, and managers at corporations, for disclosing accurate financial information about companies' operations. The Enron scandal also caused the closing of Arthur Andersen, which had been one of the Big Eight accounting firms. By 2002, following several mergers and the Andersen collapse, the Big Eight had shrunk to the Big Four. The scandals also led to the adoption of International Accounting Standards in 2003.

Computerization has also been an important driver in the growth of the accounting discipline. In 1890, Herman Hollerith developed a punch card system to automate the US Census. His company later became IBM, which introduced electronic computers in 1950. Three years later these devices supported the first automated accounting processes. The development of the first electronic spreadsheet came in 1979 with VisiCalc for the Apple II, often considered the most important PC business application ever created. Soon

Lotus 1-2-3 popularized spreadsheets on the IBM PC platform, followed by Microsoft Excel for Windows.

As the Information Age progressed, businesses have expanded the use of accounting data for strategic, marketing and research applications. Accounting systems have become more sophisticated and powerful, analyzing massive quantities of data through large-scale systems from Oracle, SAP and other global vendors. At the same time, accounting applications like Quicken and Microsoft Money now help consumers balance their checkbooks and manage their personal finances at home.

During recent years, accountants have evolved from bookkeepers tracking individual transactions into strategic consultants who help businesses of all sizes and individuals manage their finances, minimize their taxes, cut costs, and plan for the future. The increased globalization of business, greater regulatory oversight, and the need to disclose useful, accurate financial information to power capital markets, means the accounting profession is expected to continue growing for the foreseeable future.

WHERE YOU WILL WORK

ACCOUNTANTS ARE FOUND WORKING for a large number of organizations: multinational corporations; Big Four accounting firms; local, state, federal, and international governments; medium-sized businesses; auditing consultancies; hospitals; nonprofits; accounting software companies; tax preparation firms; financial institutions; and as self-employed entrepreneurs. Businesses that are too small to employ their own full-time accountants engage local CPA firms for accounting services. Families often rely on public accountants to help them file their taxes and formalize their family budgets.

A large number of accounting professionals work with the Big Four accounting firms, the major international professional services groups that provide multinational corporations with a variety of services.

The Big Four – Deloitte & Touche, PricewaterhouseCoopers, Ernst & Young, and KPMG — conduct audits and file the related regulatory reporting for most publicly traded companies. Their other services include corporate finance, and legal, actuarial, consulting, tax and related advisory services. The Big Four are not single firms, but rather networks of independent firms who work together under a common brand.

Like the Big Four, local public accounting firms provide audit, tax and management consulting services. These firms can range from larger regional practices focusing on major businesses, to one- and two-person firms that work with local businesses.

5

Every industry uses accountants, as do government agencies of all types. Accountants help retailers manage their inventories, nonprofits raise funds, governments track tax collections, software companies develop accounting applications, and sports teams maximize their ticket sales. Some accountants are generalists, while others work in such specialized areas as strategic consulting, retirement planning, and forensic accounting (helping law enforcement agencies uncover white collar crime and fraud). They also teach in high schools, colleges and universities, training the next generation of accounting professionals.

There are more than 1.2 million accountants, auditors and similar professionals working today. More than 35 percent of them are employed by accounting, tax preparation, bookkeeping and payroll services. The second-highest employment area for accountants is management of companies and enterprises, followed by local government; state government; and management, scientific and technical consulting services.

The largest concentration of accounting and auditing positions is found in the major metropolitan centers of New York and California. The top paying localities for accountants are New York City; Newark, New Jersey; Nassau County, New York; and San Francisco and San Jose, California. The states with the highest employment levels are California, New York, Texas, Florida and Pennsylvania. However, there are accounting positions available in cities and companies of all sizes across the United States.

Work environments for accountants are often the most favorable in the business world. Most work in modern, clean, safe, and environmentally-friendly offices with high-speed computers and sophisticated applications. Some work from their homes, either telecommuting if they work for corporations, or traveling to client locations if they are CPAs. Government auditors may also travel extensively to visit companies where they review financial records.

Even during economic downturns, there are always opportunities for accountants to work with businesses, governments and wealthy individuals. Accountants work everywhere that people and organizations need to manage their money – which includes virtually every enterprise and family.

THE WORK YOU WILL DO

ACCOUNTANTS ARE PROFESSIONALS who record, interpret and communicate the financial status of a company, government entity or family. Accountants prepare and examine financial records, ensuring that those records are complete and accurate, and that they comply with applicable laws and regulations.

Accountants calculate the amount of taxes owed and make sure they are paid promptly and correctly. For corporations and governments, they help ensure that financial operations are running efficiently, making suggestions for methods that improve revenues and profits while keeping costs as a minimum. Accountants provide financial data to managers, stockholders, creditors, investors and regulators so they can better evaluate the performance of an organization.

Numbers play an essential role in the daily work of accountants. They record transactions in ledgers (usually computerized) and summarize those financial activities in financial statements prepared at intervals throughout the year. Accounting professionals accumulate data about sales, income, expenses, and the tax consequences of a company's activity. They prepare financial reports and budgets, analyze information, and make sure any documents created from fiscal data are correct.

Some accountants are employed full time by corporations, government agencies, nonprofits, and other organizations. They may audit the company's financial records to verify the accuracy of the "books" (digital records on computers but still called books). They may also provide advice in such areas as risk management and assurance services (improving the quality of fiscal information).

Other accountants are self-employed or work for CPA firms, handling the work of a number of clients.

Accountants also teach in colleges and universities.

There are four major types of accountants in the workforce. The first three may be employees or outside consultants. The four types are:

Public Accountants

Public accountants provide companies and individuals with a variety of services, including filing taxes, preparing financial statements, and auditing a company's fiscal books. Public accountants (who often hold a CPA designation) may work for themselves or through an accounting firm. They may specialize in taxation, retirement planning, investments, government regulations, or forensic accounting (investigating fraud and other white collar crimes).

Management Accountants

Management accountants track and analyze financial information for companies. They prepare reports, charts, graphs and other documents for use by the management team at a company. Members of this group may also be called cost, managerial, industrial or corporate accountants.

Auditors

Auditors review financial documents to verify the information and to ensure they have been prepared properly. Both internal auditors (company employees) and external auditors (consulting accountants) make sure the funds of a company or government entity are being managed correctly. They also make suggestions to improve existing accounting processes, eliminate wasteful practices and prevent fraud.

Government Accountants

Accountants working for the government maintain the financial records of state, local or federal government entities. They often serve in auditing roles, making sure private and public organizations and individuals comply with tax laws and other regulations.

All types of accountants spend most of their time working with numbers and reports. The work is done before a computer screen, using spreadsheets and software applications to analyze financial information and reconcile conflicting data. They prepare many different types of documents, including profit and loss statements, required tax returns, balance sheets, quarterly sales figures, and budgets and revenue forecasts that paint a picture of a company's financial condition.

Accountants also look for suggestions they can make to the management team for ways to improve the accounting process and reduce the risk of fraud. Accountants may work in such specialized areas as payroll, employee benefits, cash collections (recording and tracking income from sales), disbursements (cash payments to outside vendors), procurement and inventory (keeping up with purchases of materials), and property accounting (recording the value of land, buildings, office equipment and other assets owned by the company).

While much of this work is solitary, most accountants work in teams, so there is considerable interaction with other members of their departments and with staff in other departments. Public accountants who are self-employed or work for an accounting firm also deal directly with clients, who may be corporate managers, government agencies or individuals who need assistance with their personal taxes.

Getting Started and Advancing The accounting profession offers a number of ways to enter the industry and work your way up. The typical progression is bookkeeping, accounting clerk, accountant, and Certified Public Accountant (CPA). All these levels require workers who are expert with numbers, detailed-oriented, thorough and accurate.

Some people start their careers at the entry level position of bookkeeper or clerk. These roles require at least a high school degree and sometimes a two-year associate degree in accounting. Bookkeepers are generally responsible for accurately entering financial transactions into written records or computer programs. They may record the details of employee paychecks, sales transactions, invoice payments to vendors or, at a retail store, daily register collections. Accounting clerks perform similar duties. However, while bookkeepers perform a wide range of functions, accounting clerks generally focus on one area of the company (such as payroll or inventory).

After gaining more experience and furthering their education, some bookkeepers and accounting clerks become accountants. Most accountants need at least a four-year degree to get started in the profession. They are not as involved in the day-to-day financial transactions as bookkeepers and clerks, taking a higher level view of a company's finances. Accountants typically deal with summarized data, looking at general ledger account balances and preparing financial statements from that information. Some are generalists, while others specialize in such fields as manufacturing costs or employee benefits. Accountants may manage accounting teams that include clerks and bookkeepers, or other accountants.

Certified Public Accountant – CPA The main difference between CPAs and other accountants is the licensing requirement. In addition to typical accounting duties, CPAs may deal with the general public or make regulatory filings on behalf of corporations. Most state accounting boards require CPA candidates to have at least 150 hours of college credit (more than that usually required for a bachelor's degree), and some work experience, before they can take the CPA exam and receive a license.

CPAs command higher salaries than accountants who have not received that license. Some CPAs begin their careers dealing with the general public (through an accounting firm or through their own company), and later move out of the public arena to become employees of corporations, government agencies, banks, hospitals and other organizations. Accountants who certify financial results that are filed with the Securities and Exchange Commission are required to hold a CPA license.

Specialization

There are numerous specialties that accountants may enter, with titles and areas of responsibility varying between companies or other organizations. These include:

AP/AR accountant, working with accounts payable (payments to vendors and other outside parties) or accounts receivable (amounts owed to the company, such as client billing).

General ledger accountant, preparing monthly financial statements for corporate reporting needs.

Credit manager, determining whether clients should be extended credit, what the terms should be and how collections of overdue accounts should be handled.

Cash management or treasury accountant, responsible for the details of managing a company's cash flow.

Payroll manager, overseeing the process for paying wages, deducting taxes and complying with workplace regulations.

Management accountant, performing statistical analysis and creating reports to upper management while ensuring the company is performing efficiently.

International accountant, working and traveling around the globe handling such matters as trade treaties, multinational financial reporting, and overseas mergers and acquisitions.

Internal auditor, who verifies that various departments within a company are following accepted policies and procedures. External auditors have the same duties but are not employees.

IT auditor, software auditor or computer systems auditor, a specialized type of professional who makes sure the IT department follows the proper software systems standards.

Compliance officer, who makes sure departments are following all applicable state, national and international laws and regulations.

Tax manager, who helps the company minimize its tax bills while complying with tax regulations and filing its returns in a timely manner.

Budget manager. The budget is the company's operational plan, detailing expected costs and revenues, and how the enterprise will spend its funds. The budget manager helps prepare the budget and tracks results on a regular basis against the budget plan.

Finance manager, a seasoned executive who supervises the preparation of financial reports, cash flow and regulatory compliance.

Financial controller, chief accountant and finance director. These accountant-managers direct budget preparation, control costs, plan the schedules for audits, and generally oversee accounting functions.

Chief Financial Officer – CFO

The chief financial officer (CFO) is typically the highest-ranking accounting position in a corporation (although some companies may have their treasurer in a similar role). The CFO is ultimately responsible for all the financial activities of the company, including setting budgets and reaching corporate goals.

The CFO usually reports to the board of directors and the chief executive officer (CEO). At many organizations, the CFO sits on the board of directors and may be the second-highest ranking executive after the CEO. At a public company, the CFO and CEO must certify that financial statements filed with the Securities and Exchange Commission (SEC) are accurate. These executives can face penalties, even prison sentences, if those statements are not sound.

Other common titles for corporate accountants include staff accountant, financial analyst, controller, business analyst, tax accountant, compliance professional and financial reporting analyst.

There are also many other jobs outside the typical corporate world that accountants fill.

- **Forensic accountant, who specializes in investigating such financially-related crimes as insurance fraud, embezzlement, and deceptive securities practices. They may work directly for a law enforcement agency, an accounting firm, or a large multinational corporation.**

- **IRS criminal investigation special agent. A government employee similar to the forensic accountant, who investigates financial crimes related to the Internal Revenue Code. The IRS requires CPA certification for this job.**

- **Information technology consultant. Software companies employ accountants to help them develop financial software, identify needed modifications, monitor regulatory changes, test new features, produce system documentation, and train customers who purchase the products.**

- Financial planner. Someone who helps individuals create plans to meet such financial goals as retirement, tax planning and estate planning. While financial planners are not required to be accountants, many accountants who are already working with clients on related matters branch out into financial planning so they can offer more services.

- Partner. A management position that CPAs can rise to in an accounting firm. Partners are part owners of the company, typically managing staff and helping recruit new clients. The top tier of partners are known as managing partners (or managing directors), as their main responsibility lies with management rather than day-to-day accounting and client duties.

As these roles and many others attest, the job of an accountant has evolved from a "numbers cruncher" into a strategic consultant who proactively helps organizations of all sizes operate more efficiently.

STORIES OF ACCOUNTANTS WORKING IN THE PROFESSION

I Am an Independent Public Accountant

"I am a third-generation CPA, but I didn't come to public accountancy just because my father and my grandfather did. In fact, I spent several years trying other career options before I settled into the family business.

There was no doubt from my earliest years that I could become an accountant someday. I had the mathematical aptitude, attention to details and analytical skills that made me a natural fit. I grew up around ledgers and journals, monthly closings and year-end tax reporting, budgets and financial statements – all the details of an accountant's daily life. I knew there were no vacations during tax season, when my parents worked long into the night and every weekend. I also knew that once the April 15 tax filing deadline passed, the stress ended for a while and the rest of the year was fairly quiet.

However, I wanted to explore other possibilities to see what else the world had to offer beyond public accounting. After high school, I got my bachelor's degree in accounting and worked in the family firm while completing my CPA. Once I had my license, I left our small town and moved to Hartford, Connecticut, to work in the accounting unit of a large insurance company. I had always been interested in actuarial science. An actuary is an insurance statistician who designs products that protect individuals while ensuring a fair profit return to the company. At the insurance company, I learned about how financial companies structure their products and handle investment returns. I began taking actuarial examinations, learning the complicated mathematical formulas required for the industry.

While I liked the professional challenges of corporate work, I realized I missed working with the general public. At our family firm, I had direct contact with clients that my family had known for generations. We helped them prepare their taxes, plan for their children's education and craft plans for their own retirement. At an insurance company, I knew there were families who would benefit from the products I helped create. However, I did not have direct contact with the people who did benefit from my efforts, and I realized that was the most important part of this job to me.

So I left the insurance company after four productive years and returned to the family firm in rural Pennsylvania. Since then I have been learning the ropes of running a small business and taking on more responsibility as my grandfather begins his own retirement. Being in business for yourself takes a different set of skills than working for a large company and it holds different challenges. I enjoy what I do and feel I help someone in our community every day."

I Am a Corporate Accounting Manager "My high school guidance counselor was the first to suggest that I should pursue an accounting career. At that time, there were few women in accounting, so her suggestion caught me a little by surprise. She felt my high math grades and the results of my aptitude tests indicated accounting would be a good fit for me. I was skeptical at first, but the more I read about the skills required and the opportunities available, the more sense it made.

I started out at our local community college, pursuing a two-year associate degree in accounting and business. At that point I was still living at home, so I found a part-time bookkeeping job at a local department store. I was responsible for collecting the cash drawers at the end of the night, then balancing the registers against the money, checks and charge slips in each drawer. I would then fill out the bank deposit slips (which were verified by the accounting manager) and make sure the correct amount of change was available for each register the next morning. Looking back, that entry-level job provided me with a valuable background for accounting. Looking for missing pennies while balancing those cash drawers was great preparation for the type of detailed analysis and reconciliation I would do throughout my career!

With my associate degree, I was able to land a full-time job as an accounting clerk at an industrial facility that manufactured air conditioners. My employer encouraged higher education and helped pay my tuition. This allowed me to go to night school to earn a bachelor's degree in accounting, plus prepare for the CPA exams after graduation. When I finally received my CPA license, I truly felt I was a full-fledged accountant.

My next job was as a cost accountant at an airline. Transportation is a highly competitive industry, so keeping costs as low as possible without sacrificing quality is a high priority. Our unit helped reduce costs by 30 percent over a two-year period, giving us one of the lowest cost-per-passenger-seat ratios in the industry.

My work in the cost control unit opened doors that brought me executive attention and allowed me to move into management accounting, which deals with higher-level financial analysis and reporting. We analyze data across the company, report on trends. and recommend efficiency improvements to the high level executives. After two years in this department, I was promoted to a management position, leading a team of a dozen accountants who are responsible for all of the airline's management accounting functions.

I'm not sure how much higher I want to climb the corporate ladder. I have a family now, and the higher you go in this company, the more stress you have and the less personal time is available. Wherever I end up, I will always be grateful to the attention to detail I learned balancing cash register drawers at that department store – and to the high school counselor who suggested I pursue a career in accounting."

PERSONAL QUALIFICATIONS

TECHNICAL KNOWLEDGE AS WELL AS personal strengths are the keys to building a successful career in accounting. You can begin learning about the discipline of accounting in high school, expand your knowledge in college, and enhance it through on-the-job experience and training.

A number of personal traits can also help ensure your success. Honesty, reliability and a strong sense of integrity are mandatory for an accountant in any setting. Accountants have a personal and professional duty to provide unbiased advice to clients that protects their money and ensures compliance with relevant laws. You will also be dealing with confidential information about the finances of individuals and companies, so you must keep those facts and figures private.

Accountants also need strong mathematical skills, as the majority of the work involves applying numbers to business and personal financial situations. Good technology skills also come into play with spreadsheets, databases and accounting software. While computers may handle most of the complicated calculations, you still need to understand statistics and advanced mathematics so you can determine whether those computer-generated results are correct. You also need to be analytical and creative so you can identify problems and propose solutions to address financial challenges. A good sense for how business works also helps you better serve your clients.

Being organized and detail-oriented is also critical. A good eye for details will help you find a misplaced decimal point or an incorrect numeral in a column of figures — plus help you plan how to prevent such mistakes in the future. Good time management skills help you keep your projects on track, particularly when you must multitask across several activities simultaneously or juggle a dozen clients during tax season. Accountants must learn to work within highly structured systems, corporate environments and regulatory constraints. You will need to understand and follow directions, rules, and procedures (particularly those arising from state and federal laws).

Interpersonal skills – particularly good writing and speaking communications skills — are also vital. Whether you are a self-employed CPA, part of an accounting firm or working in a major corporation, you will spend some portion of your time dealing with people from various backgrounds. The tasks accountants work on may often be solitary, but they are also team members who must interact well with others. You may make presentations to prospective clients or members of your executive board. Good writing ability will also come into play, whether you are composing emails, reports or formal regulatory filings.

Effective communications skills help ensure that your co-workers, managers and clients understand the issues and solutions you are addressing. You will need leadership and conflict resolution skills if you move into roles where you manage projects or supervise other staff members.

Finally, you will need to stay current with the financial industry. The accounting environment is constantly changing, particularly with new government regulations and tax laws that have accounting implications. If you are someone who likes to learn and stay on top of new developments, you will bring a significant advantage to your accounting career.

ATTRACTIVE FEATURES

ACCOUNTING IS A FIELD FILLED WITH opportunities. The industry features a broad, active job market with good pay and secure, stable jobs. Even entry level positions can provide salaries of $50,000 or more for the right candidates. Experts forecast double-digit growth in employment for accountants and auditors through the end of the decade. Companies and families will always need help with their taxes, plus advice on tackling other financial challenges (saving for college, buying/selling a house, retirement planning, for example). Several recent national surveys rank accounting among the top five careers available to young people.

Accountants working for large corporations typically enjoy solid job security, with opportunities to move up within their company or move on to new employers to advance their careers. While tough economic times may impact smaller accounting firms or independent CPAs, accountants are seldom out of work for long periods of time. The demand for accountants remains strong across the country and there is plenty of mobility, both in terms of geographic relocation and moving into new industries. Accounting practices vary little from one type of company to another, so the learning curve at a new employer is lower than in most occupations. Opportunities exist in private industry, corporations large and small, accounting firms, government offices, not-for-profit organizations, colleges and universities, and tax preparation offices.

If you are good at math and like working with people, solving puzzles, and finding creative solutions to business problems, you should find this career fulfilling. Your work will have a positive impact on your community and the success of your clients. A career in accounting brings financial rewards as well as personal fulfillment, professional growth, and a sense of satisfaction from helping others to better manage their money.

Accountants work indoors in pleasant offices or from their homes, and there is little physical activity required. Companies that employ accountants provide competitive salaries and attractive benefits (such as health insurance, pensions, profit sharing, paid holidays and vacations). They provide comfortable offices, modern equipment and on-the-job training to attract and retain the best candidates for their workplace.

Most organizations offer employees a well-defined path towards career advancement, including rising to such high- ranking positions as chief financial officer, treasurer or partner in a CPA firm. In smaller companies, accountants work directly with business executives and families to help them meet their financial needs. Also at a small firm, new employees can be promoted quickly as they take on increasing levels of responsibility. Accountants who go into business for themselves and start their own firms can also build lucrative practices.

Over the long term, you may decide to climb the corporate ladder into leadership roles, go into business for yourself as an independent CPA, work for a government regulatory body, teach at a university, or move into non-accounting roles at your company. Whether you spend your career as an accountant or use the practice as a stepping stone to other goals, you can reap the rewards of an accounting background for many years to come.

UNATTRACTIVE FEATURES

WHILE ACCOUNTING CAN BE A rewarding career, it is typically demanding and stressful. The detailed nature of the work means there is a high potential for human error. Working with numbers for long periods of time can become tedious, so you will need to diligently maintain your concentration to avoid costly mistakes. Accountants who audit public companies must sign statements certifying those companies have complied with all applicable laws, and accountants can face penalties or prison sentences if they deliberately miss the signs of fraud or corporate dishonesty.

Accountants work long hours – particularly those involved with preparing taxes, which keeps them busy from January until April 15 each year during "tax season." Corporate accountants and those working for large accounting firms may also be busy during peak business times, such as a complex merger deal. Large firms in particular expect new employees to prove themselves during their first three years by working nights and weekends on projects with aggressive deadlines. Working 50 hours a week or more is common for new hires (and for established CPAs in private practice). For government auditors, for example, extensive travel may be required to visit companies and review their books. Accountants at a company are often required to be in the office during the regular end-of-month closing process, plus quarterly and year-end closings. Those long hours and absences from home can make it difficult to balance your career with your personal and family life.

While accountancy does offer job security and plenty of opportunities, it is also a competitive market with many other accountants seeking the top jobs. You can enter the field with a bachelor's degree, but your prospects will be better if you can add a graduate degree and/or a prestigious certification such as CPA to your résumé.

Accountants also need regular education after college to keep up with new regulations and changing business practices, and to obtain (and maintain) their professional certifications. For example, most states require accountants to take at least 20 hours of continuing education annually (and a total of 120 every three years) to renew their licenses. Some employers offer in-house education or pay for external training for new hires. Smaller firms may expect you to schedule (and pay for) your own training. Working with state-of-the-art computers and applications also requires that you learn how to use new hardware and software, which can become frustrating and time consuming.

Work within the financial services industry is complex and sometimes exhausting. The long hours you put in over a long period of time may cause personal stress or even job burnout. Also, as with any career, you may have to

18

deal with demanding managers, unreasonable customers, uncooperative colleagues, personality conflicts, constantly-changing government regulations, office politics, and similar challenges.

Accountants work at desks in indoor offices and are not exposed to hazardous working conditions. However, spending most of your time at a computer at your desk can become boring and exhausting. The extended stress arising from long hours and lack of physical exercise can easily lead to a sedentary lifestyle that affects your overall health and fitness. Frequent computer use can also lead to back pain, eye strain, exhaustion, and repetitive motion injuries such as carpal tunnel syndrome.

EDUCATION AND TRAINING

MOST ACCOUNTANTS, AUDITORS, financial analysts and similar professionals need at least a bachelor's degree to land that first job. However, some begin their career in junior accounting positions, such as bookkeeper, assistant auditor or accounting clerk. These employees normally have a two-year associate degree in accounting or a related discipline. After working for a few years, they may go back to school and complete their four-year degree to help them move up to an accountant position.

Accountants typically obtain their bachelor's college degree in accounting or a related business field. A college degree is sufficient to get in the door at most companies. However, some firms prefer applicants with a master's degree in accounting, or those with a graduate degree in business administration (Master of Business Administration – MBA) and a concentration in accounting. Similarly, most jobs at the managerial and executive level will require a higher degree.

Colleges and universities of all sizes offer accounting degrees. Some also offer specialized programs, such as a bachelor's degree in internal auditing. Colleges also often help students get on-the-job experience through internships or part-time jobs with accounting firms and businesses. Many universities also offer a 150-hour curriculum that combines a bachelor's and master's degree in a five-year program that prepares students to become a CPA.

Recent surveys rank the top accounting schools in the country as:

University of Texas-Austin

University of Illinois Urbana/Champaign

Brigham Young University-Provo

University of Southern California

University of Michigan-Ann Arbor

University of Pennsylvania

Indiana University-Bloomington

New York University

Ohio State University-Columbus

Notre Dame

University of California-Berkley

Cornell

Tulsa

Richmond

Southern Methodist

Wake Forest

Tulane

After receiving a bachelor's degree, many students choose to pursue a master's of business administration (MBA) in accounting. An accounting MBA prepares you for the CPA exam and upper level jobs in business accounting administration. The accounting MBA also prepares students to become auditors, financial managers, and similar financial roles.

Top business schools for accounting graduate degrees are ranked:

University of Texas-Austin (McCombs)

University of Pennsylvania (Wharton)

University of Illinois-Urbana/Champaign

University of Chicago (Booth)

University of Michigan-Ann Arbor (Ross)

Stanford University

Brigham Young University (Marriott)

University of Southern California (Marshall)

New York University (Stern)

University of North Carolina-Chapel Hill (Kenan Flagler)

Many decide to become a Certified Public Accountant (CPA). The CPA designation is required for any accountant who files reports with the Securities and Exchange Commission (SEC). Even accountants who do not expect to work for publicly-traded companies become a CPA to enhance their career path within a corporation or to help them attract clients to a small firm or individual practice.

Becoming a CPA means passing a rigorous four-part national exam and meeting various requirements in the state where you will be licensed. CPAs are licensed by the state Board of Accountancy where they practice. Most states require CPA candidates to complete 150 semester hours of college (more than the typical 120 hours needed to graduate with a bachelor's degree). A small number of states allow candidates to count their years working as public accountants as an alternative to obtaining a college degree. CPAs are also usually required to log a certain number of continuing education hours to keep their CPA license in force.

While the CPA is the best known certification, there are a number of other designations available for accountants. Some indicate a focus on specific industries, while others are earned when the applicant focuses on a particular subset of the accounting profession. Those certifications and accreditations include:

Certified Management Accountant (CMA), which focuses on corporate areas such as compliance, strategy and financial analysis.

Enrolled Agent (EA), a federal government license for accountants who represent their clients in tax matters before the Internal Revenue Service.

Certified Internal Auditor (CIA)

Certified Fraud Examiner (CFE)

Certified Financial Manager (CFM)

Certified Government Financial Manager (CGFM)

Certified Information Systems Auditor (CISA)

Certified Bank Auditor (CBA)

Certified Government Auditing Professional (CGAP)

Certified Financial Planner (CFP)

Accredited Business Accountant (ABA)

Accredited Financial Examiner (AFE)

Accredited Tax Advisor (ATA)

Certified Financial Services Auditor (CFSA)

Certified Forensic Accountant (CFA)

Forensic Certified Public Accountant (FCPA)

These designations are provided by a number of professional organizations. For example, the Institute of Management Accountants offers the CMA designation, and the Institute of Internal Auditors oversees the CIA program. The American Institute of CPAs also offers additional certifications to its members, such as Certified Information Technology Professional (CITP) and Personal Financial Specialist (PFS).

EARNINGS

THE MEDIAN ANNUAL SALARY FOR accountants and auditors is about $65,000. That salary equates to an hourly rate of about $30. Only a few years ago, the average was about $60,000, so the trend is clearly upward.

The lowest earning 10 percent of accountants and auditors earn less about $40,000 annually, while the top 10 percent receive more than $110,000. Some 20 percent of the 1.2 million people employed in this profession work more than 40 hours per week, particularly during tax or budget seasons.

A recent survey by the National Association of Colleges and Employers (NACE) found that accounting students graduating this year will receive starting salaries averaging about seven percent higher than just one year ago. The NACE Salary Survey found that the average accounting graduate today is offered a starting salary of about $53,000. By comparison, the overall starting salary for college graduates is about $45,000.

The top-paying sectors for accounting graduates are professional, scientific and technical services; and finance and insurance. New graduates in these areas can start at more than $55,000.

The top paying geographic areas for accountants include the metropolitan New York City area, northern and southern California, and the San Francisco-San Jose region of northern California.

Employment opportunities have other financial considerations beyond starting salary. Benefits can vary widely from company to company. At a large corporation, benefits may add an additional 30 percent to the value of the base salary. Company benefits generally include medical and life insurance; annual bonuses; paid time off for vacation, holidays and medical leave; pensions and other retirement features; and opportunities to invest in the company's stock. Benefits at small firms may be somewhat less generous but still competitive with similar employers.

OPPORTUNITIES

EMPLOYMENT OF ACCOUNTANTS, auditors and similar professionals is forecast to grow by over 15 percent in the coming decade. The total number of accountants and auditors is expected to increase from 1.2 million to 1.4 million.

With the financial scandals and the global recession of the early 21st century, the accounting profession has received more attention. The resulting new laws and regulations, especially in the financial sector, are going to strengthen the demand for accounting services. Tighter lending standards in the wake of the recent recession will require additional auditing of borrowers, so that they can demonstrate their creditworthiness. The global economy is also expected to drive further demand for services related to international trade and international mergers and acquisitions. Economic growth, retirement of current accountants, and increased financial regulation are also expected to spur continued demand for these professionals to work with private and public entities.

Accountants with their CPA and other professional designations are expected to have the best employment prospects. Applicants with an MBA or a master's in accounting should also have an advantage in finding the best jobs.

An improving economy has boosted business at accounting firms by up to 10 percent, according to media reports, with the accounting sector regaining almost 90 percent of the jobs lost when the recession began. Businesses with increased activity are hiring more staff, including more accountants. Recent accounting graduates received the highest pay offers at the Big Four accounting firms, where signing bonuses and salaries can exceed $60,000 during the first year of employment. Local firms often do not give signing bonuses, with small accounting houses typically offering new graduates salaries in the mid-$40,000 range, surveys indicate.

Despite the poor economy in recent years, there have been numerous job opportunities for accountants. Those include public accountants at CPA firms, forensic accountants who help law enforcement agencies solve criminal cases, auditing positions with government agencies, and in-house accounting positions at large and medium-sized corporations. There is also continuing demand for accountants to help families and small businesses file their taxes.

The states with the highest percentage of employment for accountants and auditors are California, New York, Texas, Florida and Pennsylvania. The metropolitan areas with the most jobs (and most opportunities) are New York

City, Los Angeles, Washington, Chicago, Houston, Atlanta, Boston, Philadelphia, Dallas, and Denver.

GETTING STARTED

ARE YOU READY TO PURSUE A CAREER in accounting? Making the decision to learn more is a great way to start. Begin by gathering more detailed information about the profession. Whether you want to work as a public accountant or in a corporate office in a particular industry, narrowing down the specific role you desire will help you focus your energy and studies.

Next, determine how you can begin working towards your goal now. Take high school classes that will lay the foundation for your college years. There is plenty of information on accounting available at your local library, through professional associations, from colleges and universities, from guidance counselors at your high school, and on the Internet. The business sections of local and national newspapers routinely feature articles on the accounting industry.

Once you determine where to focus your attention, look for colleges and universities that provide the training you will need. Consider how you could get some entry-level experience to help you land your first job. Are there accounting internships available where you live or near the school you are considering? Could you spend a summer working as a bookkeeper or accounting clerk? Opportunities such as these can provide valuable experience and demonstrate your commitment when a potential employer reviews your résumé.

Spend some time talking to people who already work in accounting. Ask what skills, training, and experience are most helpful when accounting candidates seek that first paying position. You can find these individuals through professional associations, at job fairs, and by contacting the human resources department at local institutions. Professional associations can provide a great deal of information on the accounting profession in general, as well as local scholarship programs, internships and part-time jobs.

Consult with your personal network of family and friends for support and advice. Discuss your plans to get input on whether accounting sounds like an appropriate career choice for you. Your high school counselor can also share helpful information about local educational, employment, and networking opportunities.

Once you gather your data, it's time to give careful thought to whether accounting seems like the right choice for you. Are you comfortable dealing with numbers, statistics and financial spreadsheets? Do you communicate well with fellow students and teachers, in both the spoken and the written word? Can you handle working long hours while tackling complex problems in front of a computer screen? Would you feel confident helping major corporations make multimillion-dollar decisions, or helping families save a few dollars on their taxes?

The most important determination is whether you can see yourself enjoying the life of an accountant. If so, take your first steps today toward a rewarding, fulfilling career!

PROFESSIONAL ASSOCIATIONS

- **AACSB International**
  www.aacsb.edu

- **AICPA**
  www.aicpa.org

- **American Accounting Association**
  www.aaahq.org

- **American Association of Finance & Accounting**
  www.aafa.com

- **American Woman's Society of CPAs**
  www.awscpa.org

- **CFA Institute**
  www.cfainstitute.org

- **CFO Magazine**
  www.cfo.com

- **Institute of Internal Auditors**
  www.theiia.org

- **Institute of Management Accountants**
  www.imanet.org

- **ISACA**
  www.isaca.org

- **National Society of Accountants**
  www.nsacct.org

- **National Association of Personal Financial Advisors**
  www.napfa.org

- **National Association of State Boards of Accountancy**
  www.nasba.org

- **Women in Insurance & Financial Services**
  http://www.wifsnational.org

PERIODICALS

- **Accounting and Business**
  www.accaglobal.com

- **Accounting Today**
  www.accountingtoday.com

- **Bloomberg**
  www.bloomberg.com

- **CPA Magazine**
  www.cpataxmag.net

- **CPA Practice Advisor**
  www.cpapracticeadvisor.com

- **Financial Advisor**
  www.fa-mag.com

- **Financial Times**
  www.ft.com

- **Investor's Business Daily**
  www.investordaily.com

- **Journal of Accountancy**
  www.journalofaccountancy.com

- **Journal of Corporate Accounting and Finance**
  www.wiley.com

- **New Accountant**
  www.newaccountantusa.com

- **Practical Accountant**
  www.accountingtoday.comprc_issues

- **Wall Street Journal**
  www.wsj.com

WEBSITES

- **Accounting Coach**
  www.accountingcoach.com

- **The American College**
  www.theamericancollege.edu

- **Careers in Finance**
  www.careers-in-finance.com

- **Financial Industry Regulatory Authority**
  www.finra.org

- **Investopedia**
  www.investopedia.com

- **National Business Institute**
  www.nbi-sems.com

- **US Securities and Exchange Commission**
  www.sec.gov

- **Web CPA**
  www.media.webcpa.com

www.ingramcontent.com/pod-product-compliance
Lightning Source LLC
Chambersburg PA
CBHW071603170526
45166CB00004B/1776